ESSENTIAL SONGS FOR

trombone

Available for
FLUTE, CLARINET, ALTO SAX, TENOR SAX, TRUMPET,
HORN, TROMBONE, VIOLIN, VIOLA, CELLO

ISBN 978-1-4234-5537-0

Visit Hal Leonard Online at
www.halleonard.com

CONTENTS

ALL SHOOK UP

TROMBONE

Words and Music by OTIS BLACKWELL
and ELVIS PRESLEY

ALL THE WAY

from THE JOKER IS WILD

TROMBONE

Words by SAMMY CAHN
Music by JAMES VEN HEUSEN

AND I LOVE HER

TROMBONE

Words and Music by JOHN LENNON
and PAUL McCARTNEY

ANYONE CAN WHISTLE

from ANYONE CAN WHISTLE

TROMBONE

Words and Music by
STEPHEN SONDHEIM

Slowly and tenderly

AUTUMN LEAVES

TROMBONE

English lyrics by JOHNNY MERCER
French lyrics by JACQUES PREVERT
Music by JOSEPH KOSMA

Slowly, with expression

BABY, I LOVE YOUR WAY

TROMBONE

Words and Music by
PETER FRAMPTON

BACK AT ONE

TROMBONE

Words and Music by
BRIAN McKNIGHT

BEAUTIFUL

TROMBONE

Words and Music by
LINDA PERRY

BECAUSE OF YOU

TROMBONE

Words and Music by KELLY CLARKSON,
DAVID HODGES and BEN MOODY

BENNIE AND THE JETS

TROMBONE

Words and Music by ELTON JOHN
and BERNIE TAUPIN

BLESS THE BROKEN ROAD

TROMBONE

Words and Music by MARCUS HUMMON,
BOBBY BOYD and JEFF HANNA

D.S. al Coda

CODA

BORN FREE

from the Columbia Pictures' Release BORN FREE

Words by DON BLACK
Music by JOHN BARRY

TROMBONE

BRING HIM HOME

from LES MISÉRABLES

TROMBONE

Music by CLAUDE-MICHEL SCHÖNBERG
Lyrics by ALAIN BOUBLIL and HERBERT KRETZMER

BREATHE

TROMBONE

Words and Music by HOLLY LAMAR
and STEPHANIE BENTLEY

Moderately fast

BYE BYE LOVE

TROMBONE

Words and Music by FELICE BRYANT
and BOUDLEAUX BRYANT

CALIFORNIA GIRLS

TROMBONE

Words and Music by BRIAN WILSON
and MIKE LOVE

CAN YOU FEEL THE LOVE TONIGHT
from Walt Disney Pictures' THE LION KING

TROMBONE

Music by ELTON JOHN
Lyrics by TIM RICE

THE CHICKEN DANCE

TROMBONE

By TERRY RENDALL
and WERNER THOMAS

CLIMB EV'RY MOUNTAIN

from THE SOUND OF MUSIC

TROMBONE

Lyrics by OSCAR HAMMERSTEIN II
Music by RICHARD RODGERS

Majestically

CRAZY LITTLE THING CALLED LOVE

TROMBONE

Words and Music by
FREDDIE MERCURY

COMPLICATED

TROMBONE

Words and Music by AVRIL LAVIGNE,
LAUREN CHRISTY, SCOTT SPOCK
and GRAHAM EDWARDS

D.S. al Coda

CODA

CROCODILE ROCK

TROMBONE

Words and Music by ELTON JOHN
and BERNIE TAUPIN

Upbeat Rock

DANCING QUEEN

TROMBONE

Words and Music by BENNY ANDERSSON,
BJORN ULVAEUS and STIG ANDERSON

Strong Rock

small notes optional

DON'T KNOW WHY

TROMBONE

Words and Music by
JESSE HARRIS

DREAM LOVER

TROMBONE

Words and Music by
BOBBY DARIN

DROPS OF JUPITER
(Tell Me)

TROMBONE

Words and Music by PAT MONAHAN,
JIMMY STAFFORD, ROB HOTCHKISS,
CHARLIE COLIN and SCOTT UNDERWOOD

Moderately

D.S. al Coda

CODA

DUST IN THE WIND

TROMBONE

Words and Music by
KERRY LIVGREN

EASTER PARADE

from AS THOUSANDS CHEER

TROMBONE

Words and Music by
IRVING BERLIN

ENDLESS LOVE

TROMBONE

Words and Music by
LIONEL RICHIE

FEVER

TROMBONE

Words and Music by JOHN DAVENPORT
and EDDIE COOLEY

FIRE AND RAIN

TROMBONE

Words and Music by
JAMES TAYLOR

Slowly

THE FIRST CUT IS THE DEEPEST

TROMBONE

Words and Music by
CAT STEVENS

THE FOOL ON THE HILL

TROMBONE

Words and Music by JOHN LENNON
and PAUL McCARTNEY

Slowly

FOOTLOOSE
Theme from the Paramount Motion Picture FOOTLOOSE

TROMBONE

Words by DEAN PITCHFORD
and KENNY LOGGINS
Music by KENNY LOGGINS

FROM A DISTANCE

TROMBONE

Words and Music by
JULIE GOLD

Moderately slow

GO AWAY, LITTLE GIRL

TROMBONE

Words and Music by GERRY GOFFIN
and CAROLE KING

GOOD VIBRATIONS

TROMBONE

Words and Music by BRIAN WILSON
and MIKE LOVE

GOT MY MIND SET ON YOU

TROMBONE

Words and Music by
RUDY CLARK

A GROOVY KIND OF LOVE

TROMBONE

Words and Music by TONI WINE
and CAROLE BAYER SAGER

Moderately slow

HAPPY TOGETHER

TROMBONE

Words and Music by GARRY BONNER
and ALAN GORDON

HAPPY TRAILS
from the Television Series THE ROY ROGERS SHOW

TROMBONE

Words and Music by
DALE EVANS

Slowly

HEAVEN

TROMBONE

Words and Music by BRYAN ADAMS
and JIM VALLANCE

HEAVEN

TROMBONE

Words and Music by HENRY GARZA,
JOEY GARZA and RINGO GARZA

HELLO

TROMBONE

Words and Music by
LIONEL RICHIE

Slow Ballad

HIGH HOPES

TROMBONE

Words by SAMMY CAHN
Music by JAMES VAN HEUSEN

HOW CAN YOU MEND A BROKEN HEART

TROMBONE

Words and Music by BARRY GIBB
and ROBIN GIBB

HOW SWEET IT IS (TO BE LOVED BY YOU)

TROMBONE

Words and Music by EDWARD HOLLAND,
LAMONT DOZIER and BRIAN HOLLAND

I GOT YOU
(I Feel Good)

TROMBONE

Words and Music by
JAMES BROWN

(Spoken:) Hey!

I HOPE YOU DANCE

TROMBONE

Words and Music by TIA SILLERS
and MARK D. SANDERS

I JUST CALLED TO SAY I LOVE YOU

TROMBONE

Words and Music by
STEVIE WONDER

Moderately

I LEFT MY HEART IN SAN FRANCISCO

TROMBONE

Words by DOUGLASS CROSS
Music by GEORGE CORY

Moderately

I SHOT THE SHERIFF

TROMBONE

Words and Music by
BOB MARLEY

Moderately slow, with a beat

I WANT TO HOLD YOUR HAND

TROMBONE

Words and Music by JOHN LENNON
PAUL McCARTNEY

Moderately, with a beat

I'LL BE THERE

TROMBONE

Words and Music by BERRY GORDY,
HAL DAVIS, WILLIE HUTCH
and BOB WEST

I'LL BE

TROMBONE

Words and Music by
EDWIN McCAIN

I'M WITH YOU

TROMBONE

Words and Music by AVRIL LAVIGNE, LAUREN CHRISTY,
SCOTT SPOCK and GRAHAM EDWARDS

Moderately

IF

TROMBONE

Words and Music by
DAVID GATES

Moderately, with feeling

IF I HAD A HAMMER
(The Hammer Song)

TROMBONE

Words and Music by LEE HAYS
and PETE SEEGER

Moderately

THE IMPRESSION THAT I GET

TROMBONE

Words and Music by DICKY BARRETT
and JOE GITTLEMAN

IN THE MOOD

TROMBONE

By JOE GARLAND

IT'S A SMALL WORLD

from "it's a small world" at Disneyland Park and Magic Kingdom Park

TROMBONE

Words and Music by RICHARD M. SHERMAN
and ROBERT B. SHERMAN

IT'S TOO LATE

TROMBONE

Words and Music by CAROLE KING
and TONI STERN

ITSY BITSY TEENIE WEENIE
YELLOW POLKADOT BIKINI

TROMBONE

Words and Music by PAUL VANCE
and LEE POCKRISS

THEME FROM "JURASSIC PARK"

from the Universal Motion Picture JURASSIC PARK

TROMBONE

Composed by
JOHN WILLIAMS

KING OF THE ROAD

TROMBONE

Words and Music by
ROGER MILLER

LA BAMBA

TROMBONE

By RITCHIE VALENS

LET IT BE

TROMBONE

Words and Music by JOHN LENNON
PAUL McCARTNEY

To Coda ⊕

D.S. al Coda

CODA ⊕

LISTEN TO WHAT THE MAN SAID

TROMBONE

Words and Music by
PAUL and LINDA McCARTNEY

THE LOCO-MOTION

TROMBONE

Words and Music by GERRY GOFFIN
and CAROLE KING

Moderately

LOUIE, LOUIE

TROMBONE

Words and Music by
RICHARD BERRY

Moderate Rock

LOVE ME TENDER

TROMBONE

Words and Music by ELVIS PRESLEY
and VERA MATSON

LUCY IN THE SKY WITH DIAMONDS

TROMBONE

Words and Music by JOHN LENNON
and PAUL McCARTNEY

MAMBO NO. 5
(A Little Bit Of...)

TROMBONE

Original Music by DAMASO PEREZ PRADO
Words by LOU BEGA and ZIPPY

Relaxed two-beat feel

ME AND BOBBY McGEE

TROMBONE

Words and Music by KRIS KRISTOFFERSON
and FRED FOSTER

A MOMENT LIKE THIS

TROMBONE

Words and Music by JOHN REID
and JORGEN KJELL ELOFSSON

MY FAVORITE THINGS

from THE SOUND OF MUSIC

TROMBONE

Lyrics by OSCAR HAMMERSTEIN II
Music by RICHARD RODGERS

Lively, with spirit

THE ODD COUPLE

Theme from the Paramount Picture THE ODD COUPLE
Theme from the Paramount Television Series THE ODD COUPLE

TROMBONE

By NEAL HEFTI

Moderately, with a steady beat

ON TOP OF SPAGHETTI

TROMBONE

Words and Music by
TOM GLAZER

100 YEARS

TROMBONE

Words and Music by
JOHN ONDRASIK

ONE NOTE SAMBA
(Samba de uma nota so)

TROMBONE

Original Lyrics by NEWTON MENDONCA
English Lyrics by ANTONIO CARLOS JOBIM
Music by ANTONIO CARLOS JOBIM

PETER COTTONTAIL

TROMBONE

Words and Music by STEVE NELSON
and JACK ROLLINS

PUPPY LOVE

TROMBONE

Words and Music by
PAUL ANKA

Moderately slow

QUE SERA, SERA
(Whatever Will Be, Will Be)
from THE MAN WHO KNEW TOO MUCH

TROMBONE

Words and Music by JAY LIVINGSTON
and RAY EVANS

R.O.C.K. IN THE U.S.A
(A Salute to 60's Rock)

TROMBONE

Words and Music by
JOHN MELLENCAMP

THE RAINBOW CONNECTION
from THE MUPPET MOVIE

TROMBONE

Words and Music by PAUL WILLIAMS
and KENNETH L. ASCHER

RAINDROPS KEEP FALLIN' ON MY HEAD

from BUTCH CASSIDY AND THE SUNDANCE KID

TROMBONE

Lyric by HAL DAVID
Music by BURT BACHARACH

ROCKIN' ROBIN

TROMBONE

Words and Music by
J. THOMAS

SAILING

TROMBONE

Words and Music by
CHRISTOPHER CROSS

SEE YOU LATER, ALLIGATOR

TROMBONE

Words and Music by
ROBERT GUIDRY

Medium Shuffle (♪♪ = ⌐3¬ ♪♪)

SEVENTY SIX TROMBONES

from Meredith Willson's THE MUSIC MAN

By MEREDITH WILLSON

TROMBONE

March tempo

SHAKE, RATTLE AND ROLL

TROMBONE

Words and Music by
CHARLES CALHOUN

SHOUT

TROMBONE

Words and Music by ROLAND ORZABAL
and IAN STANLEY

SIXTEEN GOING ON SEVENTEEN

from THE SOUND OF MUSIC

TROMBONE

Lyrics by OSCAR HAMMERSTEIN II
Music by RICHARD RODGERS

Slowly, with expression

SMOOTH

Words by ROB THOMAS
Music by ROB THOMAS and ITALL SHUR

TROMBONE

SO NICE
(Summer Samba)

TROMBONE

Original Words and Music by MARCOS VALLE
and PAULO SERGIO VALLE
English Words by NORMAN GIMBEL

THE SOUND OF MUSIC
from THE SOUND OF MUSIC

TROMBONE

Lyrics by OSCAR HAMMERSTEIN II
Music by RICHARD RODGERS

SPINNING WHEEL

TROMBONE

Words and Music by
DAVID CLAYTON THOMAS

Funky, moderate Rock

SPLISH SPLASH

TROMBONE

Words and Music by BOBBY DARIN
and MURRAY KAUFMAN

STAND BY ME

TROMBONE

Words and Music by JERRY LEIBER,
MIKE STOLLER and BEN E. KING

Moderately, with a beat

SUNNY

TROMBONE

Words and Music by
BOBBY HEBB

Moderate Rock

SUPERCALIFRAGILISTICEXPIALIDOCIOUS

from Walt Disney's MARY POPPINS

TROMBONE

Words and Music by RICHARD M. SHERMAN
and ROBERT B. SHERMAN

SURFIN' U.S.A.

TROMBONE

Words and Music by
CHUCK BERRY

Solid Shuffle beat

TAKIN' CARE OF BUSINESS

TROMBONE

Words and Music by
RANDY BACHMAN

Moderate Rock

TEARS IN HEAVEN

TROMBONE

Words and Music by ERIC CLAPTON
and WILL JENNINGS

TENNESSEE WALTZ

TROMBONE

Words and Music by REDD STEWART
and PEE WEE KING

Easy Waltz

THAT'LL BE THE DAY

TROMBONE

Words and Music by JERRY ALLISON,
NORMAN PETTY and BUDDY HOLLY

THIS LOVE

TROMBONE

Words and Music by ADAM LEVINE
and JESSE CARMICHAEL

Moderate Rock

TIE A YELLOW RIBBON
ROUND THE OLE OAK TREE

TROMBONE

Words and Music by L. RUSSELL BROWN
and IRWIN LEVINE

Moderately bright

TIJUANA TAXI

TROMBONE

Words by JOHNNY FLAMINGO
Music by ERVAN "BUD" COLEMAN

Moderately

TRUE COLORS

TROMBONE

Words and Music by BILLY STEINBERG
and TOM KELLY

THE TWIST

TROMBONE

Words and Music by
HANK BALLARD

UP WHERE WE BELONG

from the Paramount Picture AN OFFICER AND A GENTLEMAN

TROMBONE

Words by WILL JENNINGS
Music by BUFFY SAINTE-MARIE and JACK NITZSCHE

WALKING IN MEMPHIS

TROMBONE

Words and Music by
MARC COHN

Moderately fast

THE WAY YOU LOOK TONIGHT

from SWING TIME

TROMBONE

Words by DOROTHY FIELDS
Music by JEROME KERN

WE ARE FAMILY

TROMBONE

Words and Music by NILE RODGERS
and BERNARD EDWARDS

Dance tempo

WE ARE THE CHAMPIONS

TROMBONE

Words and Music by
FREDDIE MERCURY

WE BUILT THIS CITY

TROMBONE

Words and Music by BERNIE TAUPIN, MARTIN PAGE,
DENNIS LAMBERT and PETER WOLF

WE'VE ONLY JUST BEGUN

TROMBONE

Words and Music by ROGER NICHOLS
and PAUL WILLIAMS

WHITE FLAG

TROMBONE

Words and Music by RICK NOWELS,
ROLLO ARMSTRONG and DIDO ARMSTRONG

A WHOLE NEW WORLD

from Walt Disney's ALADDIN

TROMBONE

Music by ALAN MENKEN
Lyrics by TIM RICE

Y.M.C.A.

TROBOMBONE

Words and Music by JACQUES MORALI,
HENRI BELOLO and VICTOR WILLIS

YESTERDAY

TROMBONE

Words and Music by JOHN LENNON
and PAUL McCARTNEY

Moderately, with expression

YOU ARE MY SUNSHINE

TROMBONE

Words and Music by
JIMMIE DAVIS

Lively

YOU LIGHT UP MY LIFE

TROMBONE

Words and Music by
JOSEPH BROOKS

YOU ARE THE MUSIC IN ME

from the Disney Channel Original Movie HIGH SCHOOL MUSICAL 2

TROMBONE

Words and Music by
JAMIE HOUSTON

Moderately fast Rock

YOU'RE BEAUTIFUL

TROMBONE

Words and Music by JAMES BLUNT,
SACHA SKARBEK and AMANDA GHOST

Moderately slow

YOU'RE STILL THE ONE

TROMBONE

Words and Music by SHANIA TWAIN
and ROBERT JOHN LANGE

YOU'VE GOT A FRIEND IN ME
from Walt Disney's TOY STORY

TROMBONE

Music and Lyrics by
RANDY NEWMAN

YOUR SONG

TROMBONE

Words and Music by ELTON JOHN
and BERNIE TAUPIN

ZOOT SUIT RIOT

TROMBONE

Words and Music by
STEVE PERRY

Spoken: Blow, dad - dy!